VERMONT WILDS

31

28

30

27

29

Lake Champlain 24

25 23

26 22

21

1	Green Mountain National Forest
2	George D. Aiken Wilderness Area
3	J. Maynard Miller Forest
4	Shaftsbury State Park
5	Canfield Fisher Memorial Pines
6	Peru Peak Wilderness Area
7	Mt. Baker
8	Lye Brook Wilderness Area
9	Big Branch Wilderness Area
10	Black Mountain
11	White Rocks National Recreation Area
12	Caves South of Woodward
13	Gifford Woods Natural Area
14	Texas Falls
15	D.A.R. State Park
16	Branbury State Park
17	Breadloaf Wilderness Area
18	Austin Brook
19	Mt. Abraham
20	Button Point Natural Area
21	Roy Mountain Wildlife Management Area
22	Groton State Forest
23	Lord's Hill Natural Area
24	Chickering Bog
25	La Platte River Marsh
26	Camel's Hump Natural Area
27	Victory Bog Wildlife Management Area
28	Lake Willoughby State Forest
29	Winooski Valley Park District
30	Sand Bar Wildlife Management Area
31	Missisquoi National Wildlife Refuge
32	Kelly Stand

20

19

15 18

17

1

_Green Mountain
National Forest_

14

16 13

12

11

9

7

6

8

5 32

1

_Green Mountain
National Forest_ 10

4

2 3

VERMONT WILDS
A FOCUS ON PRESERVATION

PHOTOGRAPHS BY
A. Blake Gardner

TEXT BY
Pauline and A. Blake Gardner

FOREWORD BY
Senator Patrick J. Leahy

A Storey Publishing Book

Storey Communications, Inc.
Pownal, Vermont 05261

Cover and interior design by Judy Eliason

Printed in the United States by New England Book Components

First Printing, April 1991

Library of Congress Cataloging-in-Publication Data

Gardner, A. Blake, 1954-
Vermont wilds : a focus on preservation /
photographs by A. Blake Gardner ; text by Pauline and A. Blake Gardner.
p.   cm.
"A Storey Publishing book" — CIP t.p. verso.
ISBN 0-88266-644-4
1. Wilderness areas—Vermont.   2. Nature conservation—Vermont.
3. Vermont—Description and travel—1981-
I. Gardner, Pauline, 1954-   . II. Title.
QH76.5.V5G37   1991   90-50414
508.743—dc20   CIP

COVER PHOTOGRAPH:
Lye Brook Falls, Lye Brook Wilderness Area

HALF-TITLE PHOTOGRAPH:
Wild Columbine,
Green Mountain National Forest.

FOREWORD

Growing up in the foothills of Vermont, we had special places that were ours and ours alone. A footpath through a patch of woods that led to a glade or clearing, where you could rest on ledges cushioned by velvet green moss and watch the tops of balsam firs, spruces, and hemlocks sway overhead.

There was the place where the brook widened and deepened — the swimming hole — or the pool where a brown trout might be laying up, just hungry enough to be tempted by the nightcrawler you were drifting by him with the current.

On hot summer days, you could lie upon the sawdust in the coolness of the icehouse (the chunks of ice cut from the surface of Lake Elmore the previous winter), spying through the loose boards at the squirrels, chipmunks, moles, and voles going about their business outside. Sometimes a whitetail buck would wander along the path, trailing some does that had gone on ahead. Not suspicious now, he would become wary later when the leaves began to fall. An occasional skunk or porcupine would crash through the undergrowth, self-assured in its natural defense against any would-be predator. As if in answer to Robert Frost's verse, "Whose woods these are," they were most emphatically theirs — yet they were ours as well.

The world seemed simpler then. Thousands of small farms kept unending tracts of rolling, green hills open for grazing and planting, checking the ever-moving forests at field's edge. It was a world where cows outnumbered people, and where everyone had a favorite place to swim and fish, hunt for mushrooms, watch the beautiful cedar waxwings cavort along a hedgerow, or catch a glimpse of a white-tailed deer.

These were commonplace experiences in the days of my youth, with natural wonders all around us. Yet our special places have been steadily shrinking, as growth and development have unleashed pressures to convert farmland and wooded hillsides into shopping centers and condominiums. The wilderness has receded under the onslaught, and the parts of Vermont so beautifully depicted in this volume are fast disappearing.

The camera can freeze the instant, capturing light and shadow, but not time. Time is unrelenting. The shadows deepen and the scene disappears. An image, so brilliantly captured today through the eye of A. Blake Gardner, may exist nowhere but on this color plate tomorrow. The camera sharpens our attention to detail, and to the fragile nature of Vermont's beauty.

I feel a kinship with Blake and Pauline Gardner: they have photographed Vermont through the eyes of my youth. This volume is an album of memories for me.

And yet, children will always be growing up in Vermont. Mr. Gardner shows us the wonders that await them, too, if we are wise enough to preserve these treasures.

Patrick J. Leahy
United States Senate
Washington, D.C.

PREFACE

On April 20, 1979, along a dusty, desert road in southeastern Arizona near the village of Portal, I first met A. Blake Gardner. My wife, Mada, and I were working in the Chiricahua Mountains with our headquarters in a cabin at Cave Creek Ranch. Blake was camping along Cave Creek about two miles above the ranch. He had hitchhiked across the United States from his home in New England, for the purpose of "seeing and studying wild America, its geography and its wildlife." A short conversation with Blake convinced us that here was a dedicated conservationist hungry for outdoor experiences and firsthand knowledge of wild creatures living far from man and his cities. Blake indicated keen interest in our work, the production of our second Peterson Field Guide, *A Field Guide to Western Birds' Nests*, for Houghton Mifflin.

We could not afford a salary, but Blake was eager to help us, so we made a deal. If he would help us find the nests and eggs that we needed to study and photograph for our book, we would feed him well. To a young man who had been living on bread and peanut butter, this sounded great. It was the beginning of a close friendship that has never wavered over the past twelve years. During the two months that we worked together daily in the desert or high in the Chiricahuas, Blake, with his youthful vigor, his determination, and his never-failing interest in the wildlife around him, especially birds, was an invaluable asset. All told, the three of us discovered 194 nests of 61 different species of birds. Blake was at my side when I photographed 25 nests that contained the eggs of 20 species.

When we headed east toward our home in Fort Lauderdale, Blake rode with us to El Paso, where he began a series of bus rides home. Until that time Blake had not owned a camera, but as soon as he reached home he bought one. In a letter he told us that the time spent with us in Arizona had encouraged him to believe that "photography would enable me to pursue goals I wanted and would also enable me to be independent, and ultimately to produce work in which I sincerely believed."

That decision, made twelve years ago, was the inception of *Vermont Wilds.* The opportunity to apprentice with photographer Paul Rocheleau on two architectural books gave Blake professional experience and a lasting friendship. Blake's horizons expanded as his photographic skill and talent became apparent. His work appeared in many newspapers and magazines, and he became photographer for several colleges and universities, including Williams College, Hartwick College, Rensselaer Polytechnic Institute, and others. Regarding this period Blake told me, "The biggest part of my education was photographing anything or anyone I could in order to make a living, learning as I went. At the time, I knew that I wanted to combine my interest in our national outdoor treasures with my photography. It just took this long for my abilities to catch up with my intentions, i.e., *Vermont Wilds.*"

While hiking through the Lye Brook Wilderness with Pauline Hellinger, who shared Blake's love of the outdoors and his interest in conservation, the idea for *Vermont Wilds* was conceived. The two of them worked together to find and photograph naturally preserved areas of Vermont and coauthored the text of this book. The relationship between Blake and Pauline became a romance, and, on July 2, 1990, they were married on the porch of our summer cottage overlooking Southwest Harbor, Maine. That day, it seemed long ago and far away that Mada and I had picked up a young hitchhiker on a dusty, desert road in Arizona.

Hal H. Harrison
Florida

ACKNOWLEDGMENTS

W
E ARE GRATEFUL for the contributions of many who have helped us to produce this book.

Above all, we thank our parents, Joyce and David Milne, and Lillian and Eric Hellinger, who have influenced and enriched our lives with passions for reading, discovery, and enjoyment of the natural world.

Without the support and enthusiasm of Hal and Mada Harrison, this book might still be a dream discussed as we hike through the wilds. The Harrisons have primed us in many ways: as mentors, teaching through example the patience and meticulous study which accompany the joys of working in the field; as authors, inspiring us with their books, reading our first draft, and encouraging us to follow through; and as friends, always willing to view photos and review copy with invaluable critiques, suggestions, and cheer.

Paul and Elaine Rocheleau have believed in this book since it was just a stack of four-by-fives. Paul has helped every step of the way with good humor, technical assistance, a sharp pencil, and an even sharper eye.

Our research began with Charles Johnson's books, *The Nature of Vermont* and *Bogs of the Northeast*, two guides which enabled us to explore and understand the state's environment.

Many people working on behalf of Vermont's natural resources, the state agencies and the U.S. Forest Service, have been generous with their assistance. John Griffith directed us to old-growth stands and sorted through National Forest Service files at the Manchester Ranger Station to furnish historic photographs.

Our search for preserved areas led us to Marc DesMeules, Director of Science and Stewardship for the Vermont chapter of The Nature Conservancy, who gave us maps, directions, and insight. He and Chris Fichtel, of the Vermont Heritage Program, marked access roads on our *DeLorme Gazetteer*, making it possible for us to find fragile and hidden places.

Harry Peet, in his last year as Executive Director of the Green Mountain Club, participated in an informative interview and pointed us toward Mt. Abraham and Camel's Hump for the big views. Richard and Barbara Ketchum took time from their important conservation work to give us valuable advice.

Special thanks are due to the staff at Storey Communications, Inc.: to John and Martha Storey, for having faith in the images and our untested writing; to Judy Eliason for her fine sense of design; and to our editor, Ben Watson, for his patience and insightful wit.

We will always remember those who have provided us with moral support and encouragement, especially Louis C. Fennell, Virginia Fetscher, Merrilee Gomillion, the Greene family, Lillian F. Healy, John and Ernie of LeClaire Custom Color, our friends at New Life Spa, and, of course, Rasalas.

INTRODUCTION

Natural beauty is Vermont's greatest resource. The forests, rivers, wetlands, and agricultural landscapes provide wildlife habitat, clean water, fresh air, and an abundance of recreational opportunities. Yet only five percent of the state is secured for future generations. The remaining rural lands are privately owned and potentially pressured by subdivision and urbanization.

Seventy million people live within an eight-hour drive of the Green Mountain State. As the regional population grows, so do the demands for natural resources and recreational areas. The prospect of a rural Vermont that both Vermonters and visitors can enjoy depends largely upon whether sizable tracts of land can be preserved while they are still available.

We set out to record the exceptional variety of ecosystems and geologic treasures that is the heart of Vermont's natural beauty, hoping that the images would stimulate admiration and concern for our wild heritage. Whether canoeing in the Missisquoi National Wildlife Refuge, hiking throughout the Green Mountain National Forest, exploring wildlife management areas and state parks, or investigating many of The Nature Conservancy's properties, each trip enriched our lives with memories and unexpected adventure.

Beyond an appreciation for spectacular scenery, we felt compelled to understand the effects of human impact on the land. Vermont was not always the lush, forested haven that we know. When Vermont conservationist George Perkins Marsh wrote *Man and Nature* in 1864, inappropriate agricultural practices and frontier attitudes had already resulted in "unremitting deterioration which seemed to erode human will, and sped the common doom of land and people." In those days, mismanagement of the countryside, based on ignorance and the fallacy of infinite resources, led to environmental destruction and economic ruin.

Today, the forests have grown back, poorer for the loss of plant and animal species. Man continues to overestimate nature's capacity to withstand abuse. Aldo Leopold's advice that, "to keep every cog and wheel is the first precaution of intelligent tinkering," is sounding more and more like the key to human survival, as scientists begin to understand the vital interdependencies of life on earth.

Vermont conservation groups express optimism in the increased environmental awareness of the last ten years. Attitudes toward the land are improving as we realize the vulnerability of the rural lifestyle that accompanies the fruitful fields, open places, mountains, and lakes which distinguish our state as a healthful place to live. Vermont products, such as maple syrup, Cheddar cheese, milk, and apples, have a deserved aura of wholesomeness which people associate with well-being.

Human health is one with the health of the land. When we travel away from home, the people we meet often assume that we live "the good life," and that Vermonters are caring, straightforward, and "down-to-earth." This perception has a basis in history. In *The Vanishing Land*, Robert West Howard writes, "Our mores, our democratic goals, our individualism, our sense of neighborliness, all have rural roots." The rural landscape provides a standard of reality, reminding us of what is genuine and enduring.

Vermont's natural beauty, and the quality of life enjoyed by those who visit or live here, are threatened by the current growth explosion. The *New England Sierran* declares that, "The 1980s will be remembered as the decade in which the forested lands of New England came under siege from land speculators and other development

interests." Irresponsible development jeopardizes the long-term
prosperity of both the land and the people by sacrificing the wealth and
integrity of our resources for short-sighted, self-perpetuating
urbanization.

As we drive through Vermont, we see the Maple Woods Shopping
Center, where asphalt replaced a majestic stand of sugar maples. We
pass the New Country car lot, which converted our rustic town into Any
Strip, U.S.A., and we feel sad remembering the trees that reached the
roadside just last month. Wendell Berry wrote in *Home Economics*,
"Obviously, the more artificial a human environment becomes, the more
the word 'natural' becomes a term of value." We worry about how the
exchange of vital habitats which benefit everyone for the self-serving
financial interests of a few will affect the future of the land and the
lifestyle that Vermonters value.

The Vermont Natural Resources Council reports that, "In Bethel,
Bolton, Burlington, and beyond, Vermonters are worried that the state's
transportation projects are speeding us toward a drastically altered
landscape and lifestyle." The wonderful, curvy roads that show us
farms, villages, magnificent views, and big sky are a refreshing
attraction in themselves. However, unnecessary road projects seem to be
straightening the Green Mountain State, bypassing the traditional
countryside that both residents and visitors cherish.

When a highway directs traffic away from the villages through
farmland and open places, Vermonters lose in two important ways:
visitors do not contribute to the economic vitality of the villages, and the
farmland becomes a target for sprawl and strip development. Once the
land's use is converted from agricultural and forestry practices to
commercial and residential development, it is truly "used," and the
effects are irreversible.

According to The Nature Conservancy, Vermont's biggest
environmental problem is the breaking up of large parcels of land,
irrespective of ecological units. Protection of plant and animal
communities often depends upon the purchase of large preserves, which
are hard to acquire once they are subdivided. Chris Fichtel of the
Vermont Natural Heritage Program explains: "An investor will purchase

land from a farmer or a timber company and then subdivide for development interests. Act 250 [the state's environmental review process] works as a preventative measure, helping to preserve species that are rare but not yet endangered."

Marc DesMeules of The Nature Conservancy comments: "We're the only species capable of recognizing that other species are endangered. Ignorance is the main cause for losing a species. While we can't tell people not to develop in a democracy, we can slow down, plan ahead, and educate individual landowners." While it may be legal to destroy life-sustaining habitats, and replace them with the ugly and the commercial, is it moral to do so? Wendell Berry articulates our concern: "We diminish the future by deeds we call *use*, but that the future will call *theft*." As a society, we need to make careful choices about the kind and the scale of changes we make as we impact the land. Both the Amish and the Kenyan peoples have a saying: "We didn't inherit the land from our parents; we are borrowing it from our children."

Enlightened people agree that we are doing grave damage to our life-sustaining ecosystems. The need for an environmentally sustainable economy is no longer in question, but at present we lack the political will to sufficiently rattle the status quo in search of real solutions, based on an understanding that it is unnatural, and even immoral, not to address environmental problems which affect all of us, as well as future generations.

In a 1990 Earth Day speech, former U.S. Senator Gaylord Nelson said that the major environmental problem today is not global warming, pollution, or even exponential population growth, but the absence of a conservation ethic: "It is the ethics and mores of a society that guide our conduct. If we were guided by a conservation ethic, we would never have done all the foolish things we've done. You didn't have to be a scientist to recognize the kind of disaster we were creating. We wouldn't drain, and continue to drain, half the wetlands of America.... We wouldn't be eroding our soil base which sustains us. Raising a generation with a conservation ethic is the most important thing we can do."

Many Vermonters are working, through education and grassroots participation, to promote and actualize a conservation ethic. Raising a "conservation generation" is one of the important goals of the Vermont Institute of Natural Science. Director Sarah B. Laughlin emphasizes the necessity of "teaching children the basic environmental facts of life, beginning with the place of humans in the natural world." VINS programs help both adults and children understand the world as a complete, integrated system, where all species have a right to live, and humans have the responsibility of protecting their habitats.

Among its many goals, the Vermont Natural Resources Council actively provides protection for habitats, education to empower citizens groups, and environmental leadership through the courts and the legislative system to improve economic policy and to promote sustainable land and energy uses. When the residents of a Vermont town needed help to preserve a "top trout stream" with the aim of securing "a sound downtown economy and clean water at the same time," they turned to the VNRC for the help they needed.

Upon reading that twenty-five percent of Vermont's working dairy farms went out of business in the last decade, we envisioned a nightmare in which painted cow plaques on lawns would soon replace Holsteins in open fields. Fortunately, The Vermont Land Trust is working with landowners to protect thousands of acres of productive lands through the use of voluntary conservation easements.

The Nature Conservancy works successfully with individuals, the state, and other groups to identify and preserve natural diversity. Land acquisition and creative stewardship agreements are employed as conservation tools to protect "lands containing the best examples of all components of our natural world." The Nature Conservancy is presently helping the Green Mountain Club to purchase and protect land on the Long Trail, the oldest long-distance trail system in the country.

These are just a few of the eighty Vermont groups that participated in the 1989 Conservation Celebration, and all are equally deserving of recognition. Vermont is a small state with a wide appeal to many interests. Those who are concerned with preserving the state's natural beauty now have a rare window of opportunity: to both inspire and provide leadership that will make healthy choices and necessary changes for the long-term health of the land and its people.

Dense fog weaving across the bog mat makes the white cedars and tamaracks vanish, then reappear. Dewdrops balance on every limb, showering us with the slightest touch. From the woods, we hear the slow, deliberate hammering of a pileated woodpecker, the scolding alarm of a red squirrel, and an ovenbird answering, "teacher, teacher, teacher."

Although it looks like solid ground, the fen is thirty feet deep, and its fragile surface undulates with every footstep. Tiptoeing onto the mat, we carefully pick our way among the delicate orchids, thin sedges, and carnivorous pitcher plants.

Chickering Bog, The Nature Conservancy

"For a great tree death comes as a gradual transformation. Its vitality ebbs slowly. Even when life has abandoned it entirely it remains a majestic thing. On some hilltop a dead tree may dominate the landscape for miles around. Alone among living things it retains its character and dignity after death. Plants wither; animals disintegrate. But a dead tree may be as arresting, as filled with personality, in death as it is in life. Even in its final moments, when the massive trunk lies prone and it has mouldered into a ridge covered with mosses and fungi, it arrives at a fitting and noble end. It enriches and refreshes the earth. And, later, as part of other green and growing things, it rises again."

EDWIN WAY TEALE
Dune Boy: The Early Years of a Naturalist

White Birch in a Wood Fern Colony, Groton State Forest

"That wildlife is merely something to shoot at or to look at is the grossest of fallacies. It often represents the difference between rich country and mere land."

ALDO LEOPOLD
A Sand County Almanac

Winter Tracks, George D. Aiken Wilderness Area

The last continental glacier scoured the narrow valley between Mt. Hor and Mt. Pisgah, blocked both ends with debris, and ultimately created one of the deepest and loveliest lakes in New England. Lake Willoughby supports a large variety of fish in cold, clean water that descends in places to more than three hundred feet.

The inaccessible cracks and folds of Mt. Pisgah's cliffs provide a safe niche for rare alpine plants, while the clifftops are vantage points for watching hawks. If the wind is right, large numbers of hawks in kettles spiral together in thermals, offering the viewer an aerial ballet staged against a blue sky.

Lake Willoughby at Dawn, Lake Willoughby State Forest

Below us, circling and twittering, chimney swifts dart after their insect prey. Suddenly, a sleek falcon comes into view, rapidly beating its wings. The falcon plunges earthward, accelerates with a few strong beats, locks wings against its body, and rockets down.

Here, atop White Rocks, we witness the spectacular hunting behavior of a rare migrant, perhaps a nesting, peregrine falcon. Against the panorama of earth and sky, the bull's-eye impact from the peregrine's closed talons knocks the swift into a spiraling tumble. With a relaxed swoop, the hunter then plucks its senseless meal out of the air.

White Rocks Cliff, White Rocks National Recreation Area

Artifacts can be found throughout Lye Brook. Crumbling stone walls brace the old train bed and prevent it from eroding down the slopes. Overgrown with roots, railroad ties remain from logging days. Below the falls, stumps of great support beams are remnants of a wooden bridge once swept away in a deluge.

Trees have grown again, yet so much life was eliminated in successive cuttings that the pleasant young woods are disquietingly uninhabited. With protection of this wilderness, after generations of time the recovering land may again mature into a flourishing forest.

Fern Hollow, Lye Brook Wilderness Area

"Industrial foresters seem to think that a commercial forest of a single tree species will meet wildlife needs as well as a natural forest of many species. Yet forests have thrived for over three hundred million years as diverse habitats. Simplifying them to suit industrial procedures could threaten the evolutionary viability not only of wildlife, but of the forests themselves."

DAVID RAINS WALLACE
Life in the Balance

Yellow Birches, Lye Brook Wilderness Area

Gleaming fiberglass boats cruise by, each armed with a dozen fishing rods.
Vermonters feel dismay in finding fouled water, a diminished fish population,
and the roar of boat traffic. Our freedom to speed across lakes and rivers
usurps the right of fish, ducks, and the wild loon to survive in their natural
habitat. If we row, paddle, or sail, and limit the use of motors on our waters,
might the fish caught taste better for the endeavor?

Winooski River Delta on Lake Champlain, Winooski Valley Park District

"To insure future supplies of lumber, wood pulp and cellulose by 'forest management' is in the best tradition of American industry. People are told that the lumber and paper companies are growing more wood than they are cutting. This happy fact relates to the growth of the *annual increments.* Seedlings, saplings, one-year of added wood rings will never restore true wildness despite appealing color advertisements of deer, beaver and bobwhites in managed forests. If forest managers wait 500 years (which they will not) will the managed forest then be the home of deer, bear, cougar, beaver and wolverine? Will there be wild flowers and berry-laden bushes? Will there be ferns, mosses and lichens, lakes, streams with trout, ponds teeming with ducks?...American wilderness is bequeathed to us only once; destroyed, it is unrestorable."

RUTHERFORD PLATT
The Great American Forest

Cottonwoods, Sand Bar Wildlife Management Area

Why is a Vermont gorge called Texas Falls? Research has revealed no clue. Perhaps the swirling waters were owned by a Texan pining for home, or a Vermonter longing for a warmer clime. Does the drainage basin resemble the shape of the Lone Star State? Perhaps the smooth, sculpted forms of bedrock are as worn and tawny as a cowboy's saddle.

When asked, a Forest Ranger declared, "No one knows." And so, this wild chasm's name remains an enigma to spur the imagination.

Texas Falls, Green Mountain National Forest

The river mirrors a violet horizon, as quivering lights slowly appear in the night. Coyote yips and howls are relayed from the velvet blackness of distant woods, and an occasional meteor sparks across the Milky Way.

At daybreak, stars merge with the oncoming brightness to display a white veneer outlining the landscape. Morning breezes shake branches, sending glistening cold dust out of the trees. As the rising sun reduces the frost to beads of water, a trail of ice-rimmed moose tracks melts into the thawing earth.

Frosted Grasses, Victory Bog Wildlife Management Area

A great horned owl with a chipmunk clutched in its powerful beak glides silently through a clearing to settle on a branch. All at once, a gang of crows swoops in. With raucous caws and much wing-flapping, they attack. The hunter bows and bends repeatedly to avoid being struck. Unable to dislodge his catch, perseverance turns to distraction, and the crows fly off.

With strong strokes of its six-foot wings, the owl lifts off to land high in the tallest white pine. Edging toward a large nest of sticks, it leans to drop the rodent inside. Without a pause, the owl disappears into a stand of red pines where a noisy squirrel chatters.

Red Pines, Roy Mountain Wildlife Management Area

Like anchored frigates, cumulus clouds float heavily on a hazy sky. Deerflies buzz drowsily, and the most delicate grasses hold still in the humidity.

In the west, white thunderheads mushroom through the darkening atmosphere. These swift-moving clouds block the sun, casting ominous shadows across the beaver meadow. On a distant ridge, a white bolt zigzags through the grey streaks of rain, followed by a faint boom. More numerous and closer now, bursts of lightning are chased by deafening bangs. A sudden downpour blurs the landscape. As the mountainous clouds briskly sail east, the tempest passes, leaving behind a patter of lingering drops. Sunbeams spotlight the mist as it rises into the cooled air above the glossy marsh.

Approaching Storm, George D. Aiken Wilderness Area

From our camp last night, we could hear chirps from migrating birds flying low over the moonlit canopy. A burst of activity in the treetops greets us in the morning, as we walk along the Lamoille River through waist-deep, dew-covered ferns. Black-and-white warblers circle branches, and black-throated green warblers flutter about, looking for worms. A red-breasted nuthatch, like a repetitious wind-up toy, peeks at us, then hides behind a limb, and, all the while, chickadees are busy minding everyone else's business.

Swamp Maples and Ferns, Sand Bar Wildlife Management Area

An intermittent stream trickles slowly down a ravine toward a stone ledge, where it creates a natural fountain. A wet rock shelf forms a chest-high basin where we douse ourselves, drinking handfuls of clean, cold water. The mountain is a generous host, refreshing us while it provides the trilliums, clintonias, and trout lilies the power to herald spring.

Red Trillium, Big Branch Wilderness Area

"Climb the mountains and get their good tidings. Nature's peace will flow into you as sunshine flows into trees. The winds will blow their own freshness into you, and the storms their energy, while cares will drop off like autumn leaves."

JOHN MUIR

Fall Leaves, Branch Pond, Green Mountain National Forest

Stinging nettles, hobblebush, slippery rocks, and hidden holes, just the size of a boot, make hiking to the boulders a bushwhacking adventure. After a few stream crossings and a vigorous climb, we reach a dramatic view. The hollow looks as though an Impressionist painter went mad with a giant brush.

Heading back, shaded by a glowing canvas of leaves, we take time to explore the rugged slopes and unnamed waterfalls. As we descend into the valley, we are pleasantly surprised by approaching zephyrs. Their scented warmth surrounds us like an invisible cloud, then passes; a sensual contrast to the crisp fall air.

Lye Brook Hollow, Lye Brook Wilderness Area

"Conservation is a state of harmony between man and land. By land is meant all of the things on, over, or in the earth. Harmony with land is like harmony with a friend; you cannot cherish his right hand and chop off his left."

ALDO LEOPOLD
A Sand County Almanac

Limestone Boulders, Caves South of Woodward, The Nature Conservancy

The high water of spring spreads from Lake Champlain and fills a flooded forest with surreal reflections. Strange, hoarse croaks come from nests hidden throughout the dense canopy, revealing Vermont's largest great blue heron rookery. These tall wading birds, like so many wild creatures, require wild places for their survival.

Silver Maples, Shad Island, Missisquoi National Wildlife Refuge

"It is interesting to contemplate a tangled bank, clothed with many plants of many kinds, with birds singing on the bushes, with various insects flitting about, and with worms crawling through the damp earth, and to reflect that these elaborately constructed forms, so different from each other and dependent upon each other in so complex a manner, have all been produced by laws acting around us."

CHARLES DARWIN
On the Origin of Species

McGinn Brook, Big Branch Wilderness Area

Not far from the summit, we come upon a frail but determined older man sharing lunch with a young boy. Sporting a sun-bleached cap with a Green Mountain Club patch over its worn visor, the man explains that they had been looking forward to climbing this mountain all winter. He says he was just about the same age as his grandson the first time he discovered the adventure of hiking the Long Trail. His weathered smile reveals pleasant memories, as he expresses hopes that this Vermont treasure will be enjoyed for generations to come.

Mt. Abraham, Green Mountain National Forest

Overhead, Orion follows night into the predawn horizon, while a thick fog blankets the distant mountains. Did the glacial ice sheets that filled Vermont's valleys appear like this mass of clouds?

The cold blue hue of shadows and shapes is suddenly transformed by sunlight pouring over the top of Big Deer Mountain. A world of color and detail emerges as the fog dissolves. Along the slopes of Owl's Head, a lone red-tailed hawk wheels in rising currents; its call is a piercing prelude to the day.

View of Lake Groton from Owl's Head, Groton State Forest

"What better gift to give our children, and our children's children, than clean water to drink, mountains to climb, and woods to walk through?"

GOVERNOR MADELEINE KUNIN

Little Mud Pond, White Rocks National Recreation Area

There's a wide hollow in the otherwise hardy old black gum tree. The pungent odor from fresh scats limits us to a quick look inside, but a few raccoon hairs snagged on the bark reveals who has been there.

Many Vermont birds and mammals need cavities in aged trees, whether downed or standing dead, for their nest or den sites. In young forests, and in most "managed" forests, these essential holes are absent, as are the species that utilize them for reproduction.

Black Gum Raccoon Den, J. Maynard Miller Forest, Town of Vernon

The shape of Vermont was determined during the Ice Age, when glaciers gouged the land and deposited material ranging from clay particles to house-sized boulders. As the ice retreated northward, cold winds whipped coarse sand across the landscape, while mounds of till lined valleys and dammed lakes. Amidst the scrubby forests, spear-bearing natives stalked huge mastodons.

The glacial ponds, rounded boulders, and great heaps of sand remain today, in a place where black bear, deer, and moose roam free.

Kettle Pond, Groton State Forest

Muddy boots and eager appetites are all we have to show for three days of hiking in the rain. Almost home, we notice the full moon starting to crest a slope that gleams with the lustre of sunset light. Determined, we pull off the road, haul the camera gear up a hill, and record the brief conjunction of glowing orb and somber mountain.

Full Moon, Green Mountain National Forest

OTTER

Gentle gurgling splash,

An undulating ripple,

A silver curve. Gone.

Haiku by MADA HARRISON

River Otter Tracks, George D. Aiken Wilderness Area

The plants growing on the summit of Camel's Hump are tough enough to tolerate severe cold, driving rain, and blasting winds. However, the footsteps of unwary hikers can easily destroy them. Rare tundra vegetation is often mistaken for a common patch of grass.

You can protect this fragile alpine community by choosing to step only on the mountaintop rocks. Few environmental safeguards are so simple.

Alpine Grasses, Camel's Hump Natural Area

Water striders dash back and forth across a shallow pool, while bumblebees drone over newly opened flowers. Electric blue dragonflies dart about, snatching insects and defending their territories. Toads bleat in search of mates. In the same brook, two mallards feed underwater, tails up, webbed feet peddling for balance. A dozen male blackbirds, bunched tightly in a swamp maple, survey the scene with clamorous calls. Abruptly, the flock rises like a puff of smoke and drifts out of sight.

Morning Dew on Grasses, George D. Aiken Wilderness Area

Beyond Devil's Hill, at the base of a steep, rocky slope, there is a small parcel of land that contains immense beeches, birches, ashes, maples, and hemlocks. Somehow, this twenty-five-acre lot was spared the industrial logging of the surrounding forest, saving old-growth specimens that hold state records.

In November, after leaves have fallen, these patriarchs stand apart from the younger woods. With mighty branches etched against a grey sky, the magnificent trees watch the approach of winter, like sentinels from a previous age.

Yellow Birch Trunk, Lord's Hill Natural Area, Groton State Forest

"A lake is the landscape's most beautiful and expressive feature. It is earth's eye; looking into which the beholder measures the depth of his own nature. The fluviatile trees next to the shore are the slender eyelashes which fringe it, and the wooden hills and cliffs around are its overhanging brows."

HENRY DAVID THOREAU
Walden

Branbury State Park from Rattlesnake Cliffs, Green Mountain National Forest

Up from the drab mat of last year's lingering leaves, bright green stripes unfurl. Nearby, wood sorrel stars decorate the ground cover. A ruby-throated hummingbird, weighing as little as a letter, completes a journey of thousands of miles, to sip at a dainty columbine. On a mild, rainy night, salamanders respond to an ancient call by migrating en masse to breeding pools.

Spring in Vermont is a time when our complex world amazes us with day-to-day changes and perennial miracles.

False Hellebore, Big Branch Wilderness Area

Aside from man, no creature in North America has altered the environment more than the beaver. Obvious signs of beaver activity are the extensive felling of trees and the damming of small streams. The resulting pond quickly forms a rich aquatic landscape that supports a wide variety of life. Eventually, the pond fills in to become a meadow, which in turn promotes the regrowth of woods.

Frozen Beaver Channel, George D. Aiken Wilderness Area

"I am convinced that man has suffered in his separation from the soil and from the other living creatures of the world: the evolution of his intellect has outrun his needs as an animal, and as yet he must still, for security, look long at some portion of the earth as it was before he tampered with it."

GAVIN MAXWELL
Ring of Bright Water

D.A.R. State Park

Each year, one hundred thousand people hike the Long Trail. Some leave their thoughts behind in logbooks at shelters along the way:

"I'll be sixty in a week, and I feel blessed to be able to experience this wonderful place!"

"This is my first trip, and I love it, because I learn something new every day."

"When I'm in the city, I feel fortunate knowing there is country left where I can find silence and my inner soul."

"I came back after a ten-year pause in hiking. Three children and my job kept me from these trails. Now the kids are grown, and I huff a little more uphill, but I'm ever so glad to be back."

"Another hike has brought my wife and me closer to each other."

"I'm cold, wet, and hungry. Funny thing is, I've never been happier."

Mt. Baker Summit, Big Branch Wilderness Area

Fossils of corals, which thrived in warm, shallow seas long before mammals, birds, or even dinosaurs appeared, can be found on Button Island. The corals existed five hundred million years before *Homo sapiens* first walked the earth.

Within these few acres of land, half a billion years of earth's history can be viewed on or in the bedrock. Fossils, glacial markings, and trees whose ancestors can be traced back to the Age of Reptiles all bear witness to the fact that nature evolved just fine before our time.

Button Island, The Nature Conservancy, Button Point Natural Area

The beech tree has a smooth grey bark and toothed leaves, which cling to the branches until spring like pale, papery moths.

Vast areas of the eastern forests were covered by beech woods before the massive cutting of the 1800s. An abundance of beechnuts sustained immense flocks of passenger pigeons — now extinct, but once the most numerous of all birds. Today, black bears, porcupine, deer, and squirrels depend on a supply of beechnuts, as do ruffed grouse, wild turkeys, and some smaller birds.

Beech Leaves, Lye Brook Wilderness Area

Glaciers, lakes, and streams have etched and sculpted Vermont into a combination of hills and valleys accented with many forms of water, giving the land a delightful character. People are drawn by the rare opportunity to listen to a brook as it tumbles down a wild gorge, or to swim in a clean lake surrounded by woods, where birds and crickets can be heard.

To whom do we trust the stewardship of these rich habitats, on which our short-term enjoyment and long-term survival depend? The recreational popularity of our resources will increase with population growth, as will our need for open space and clean water.

Horizontal Falls, Lye Brook Wilderness Area

An ancient river system carved the eccentric east-to-west course of the Lamoille River. Cottonwoods and silver maples tower above muddy swamps and fertile marshes where the Abenaki Indians once hunted and fished.

The Sand Bar Wildlife Management Area provides a vital preserve for nesting waterfowl and migrating species, since so many wetlands along the Atlantic Flyway have already been lost to development.

Lamoille River, Sand Bar Wildlife Management Area

"Into every empty corner, into all forgotten things and nooks, nature struggles to pour life, pouring life into the dead, into life itself. That immense, overwhelming, relentless, burning ardency of Nature for the stir of life!"

HENRY BESTON
The Outermost House

Fiddleheads, Big Branch Wilderness Area

"A child's world is fresh and new and beautiful, full of wonder and excitement. It is our misfortune that for most of us that clear-eyed vision, that true instinct for what is beautiful and awe-inspiring, is dimmed and even lost before we reach adulthood. If I had influence with the good fairy who is supposed to preside over the christening of all children I should ask that her gift to each child in the world be a sense of wonder so indestructible that it would last throughout life, as an unfailing antidote against the boredom and disenchantments of later years, the sterile preoccupation with things that are artificial, the alienation from the sources of our strength."

RACHEL CARSON
The Sense of Wonder

Ferns and Moss, Gifford Woods Natural Area

In an age of few genuine heroes, The Nature Conservancy has earned praise
for its leadership in the preservation of ecologically important land throughout
the United States. Over the last three decades, the Vermont chapter alone has
quietly protected more than seventy thousand acres of critical natural areas.

White Pine, Black Mountain, The Nature Conservancy

Sunlight filters through golden, orange, and maroon leaves, opening the hidden places of the forest. Migrating birds, moving south, linger to feed on the plump fruits of trees and shrubs. Mammals cache or feast on the success of the season, plants transfer energy into roots and seeds, while the accumulation of fallen leaves begins to rejuvenate the soil for next year's growth. Autumn, with its crisp air and fleeting daylight, is a time when life balances between seasons.

Fall at Kelly Stand, Green Mountain National Forest

"Flowers changed the face of the planet. Without them, the world we know —
even man himself — would never have existed. Francis Thompson, the English
poet, once wrote that one could not pluck a flower without troubling a star.
Intuitively he had sensed like a naturalist the enormous interlinking
complexity of life."

LOREN EISELEY
The Firmament of Time

Marsh Marigolds, Shaftsbury State Park

Fresh moose tracks in the soft mud along Austin Brook and a sunlit raspberry patch recently torn by a browsing bear are exciting signs that remind us that these rarely seen creatures are present.

The survival of Vermont's wildlife depends upon the preservation of more large, uninterrupted tracts of land like the Breadloaf Wilderness. As Aldo Leopold cautioned, "Wilderness is a resource which can shrink but not grow."

Austin Brook, Breadloaf Wilderness Area

How "wild" will our descendants' wilderness be without the chance to see a pair of coyotes trotting across a misty clearing, or hear haunting howls echo through darkening woods, or, if lucky, come upon a litter of pups playing king-of-the-mountain?

It's been forty years since coyotes first established themselves in Vermont. Some say coyotes fill an important and healthful niche, while others want a bounty set on the animal. Like most predators, the coyote is misunderstood. A prevailing imbalance between our human needs and our knowledge of the natural world threatens both wildlife and the rural landscape.

Coyote Tracks, George D. Aiken Wilderness Area

Frigid blasts of wind force us to huddle in a rocky niche on top of Mt. Baker. We've been on the trail since dawn, but the bleak sky makes photography impossible. Passing the time, we look south and east with binoculars, thumb through field guides, take notes, make plans, and resist the chill with steaming tea from the thermos, all the while watching for light.

As we head home down an icy trail, the sun projects below the clouds and illuminates a hardy stand of birches. Suddenly, it was gloves off, packs off, camera gear out, and our patience was rewarded.

White Birches on the Mt. Baker Trail, Big Branch Wilderness Area

Vermont's first naturalist, Samuel Williams, observed in 1809 how, "the largest part of Vermont is yet in the state in which nature placed it. Uncultivated by the hand of man, it presents to our view a vast tract of woods, abounding with trees, plants, and flowers almost infinite in number, and of the most various species and kind."

Throughout the next one hundred years, most of the woods were either cut or burned for pastures and homesites, while the rest were extensively logged. Few areas were protected. One small remnant of the colonial forests is the fragile Gifford Woods, full of woodland plants, rich soil, and monumental trees.

Sugar Maples, Gifford Woods Natural Area

In 1911, when Colonel Joseph Battell transferred ownership of one thousand acres of Camel's Hump to the State of Vermont, he insisted that the forest "be preserved in a primeval state." Thanks to the concerted efforts of several conservation groups, this 4,083-foot mountain is permanently protected, retaining the wild characteristics that have been lost on most other high peaks in Vermont.

Camel's Hump Summit, Camel's Hump Natural Area

"How many generations will pass before it will have become nearly impossible to be alone for even an hour, to see anywhere nature as she is without man's improvements upon her? How long will it be before — what is perhaps worse yet — there is no quietness anywhere, no escape from the rumble and the crash, the clank and the screech which seem to be the inevitable accompaniment of technology? Whatever man does or produces, noise seems to be an unavoidable by-product. Perhaps he can, as he now tends to believe, do anything. But can he do it quietly?

"Perhaps when the time comes that there is no more silence and no more aloneness, there will also be no longer anyone who wants to be alone."

JOSEPH WOOD KRUTCH
Grand Canyon: Today and All Its Yesterdays

Moose River, Victory Bog Wildlife Management Area

The Skyline Trail, considered to be the jewel of the Long Trail, was forged by Professor Will C. Monroe over the course of ten summers, beginning in 1916. Monroe was a botanist, an expert in Balkan languages, and the guardian of six large dogs. Contemporaries viewed him as a "colorful and irascible man with a powerful personality." These qualities, and his great love for the Green Mountains, motivated him to organize and pay for a trail-building crew, consisting of friends from New York and New Jersey who shared his passion for Vermont.

In place of an overgrown, unsafe path, with tame and monotonous grades, Monroe fulfilled the Green Mountain Club's dream for "a high, scenic mountain pathway" by creating a spectacular route across the mountain he called The Couching Lion.

Camel's Hump from the Dean Trail, Camel's Hump State Forest

"First, we should not forget that the remnant of original America that now remains is also a large part of all the wilderness that remains anywhere on earth. What we possess is a unique treasure for people everywhere.

"Second, we should remember that wilderness is more than interesting vacation land. It represents spiritual and aesthetic values measurable by the song of birds, by an abundance of wildlife, by sunsets, and by the music of conifers. We may well discover in the wilderness, and in our attitude towards it, many of the essentials for survival itself."

JUSTICE WILLIAM O. DOUGLAS
This Is the American Earth

Victory Bog Wildlife Management Area

Nestled at the base of Mt. Horrid's cliff is a small pond. The resident beaver checks the stick-and-mud dam for leaks before diving into his lodge for the day. On a bleached limb, a belted kingfisher perches, motionless, waiting for a fish to swim within range. Iridescent green-and-white tree swallows circle high, then fly low, skimming the pond's surface for insects.

Sun beams between the valley walls, sidelighting the bouldered slope where a moose and her calf emerge. Testing the air with her bulbous nose, looking around carefully, the mother wades into the water. Both stand belly-deep, drinking and looking. Then, one behind the other, the moose depart, climbing steadily up the steep terrain.

Mt. Horrid Birches, Green Mountain National Forest

"What I have been preparing to say is this, in wildness is the preservation of the world ... Life consists of wildness. The most alive is the wildest. Not yet subdued to man, its presence refreshes him ... When I would re-create myself, I seek the darkest wood, the thickest and most interminable and, to the citizen, most dismal swamp. I enter as a sacred place, a *Sanctum sanctorum.* There is the strength, the marrow, of Nature. In short, all good things are wild and free."

HENRY DAVID THOREAU
Essay on "Walking" (1851)

Erratics near Kettle Pond, Groton State Forest

George D. Aiken was the kind of common-sense, make-do, independent thinker that we would like all politicians to be. One of his proudest achievements was the Eastern Wild Areas Act, passed in 1974, which set aside land in our national forests to be kept in a primitive state.

Senator Aiken saw rising land values and opposition from those who made their fortunes exploiting natural resources as the two biggest threats to the preservation of unspoiled places. His success in doing the right thing for the long run was explained by Vermont historian Ralph Nading Hill: "He could be everybody's man because he was nobody's man but his own."

Winter Still Life, George D. Aiken Wilderness Area

"What we have saved and what we *will* save in the next few years will be all that will remain to be passed on to future generations. There will never be another chance."

THE NATURE CONSERVANCY

Hairy Beardtongue, Button Point Natural Area

Yesterday was chilly, but today is frigid with the kind of bitter cold that numbs through thick mittens and boots. Nothing moves on this silent dawn; life remains frozen or snugly hidden.

Returning to a beaver channel, which was glasslike yesterday, we discover the most fragile ice crystals have blossomed. As the sun spills over the spruces, bathing the delicate patterns in light, the crystals slowly fade, then vanish. Only in this contrary season, on rare Siberian nights, do these icy flowers grow.

Ice Crystals on a Beaver Channel, George D. Aiken Wilderness Area

"History tells us that earlier civilizations have declined because they did not learn to live in harmony with the land. Our successes in space and our triumphs of technology hold a hidden danger; as modern man increasingly arrogates to himself dominion over the physical environment, there is the risk that his false pride will cause him to take the resources of the earth for granted — and to lose all reverence for the land."

STUART UDALL
The Quiet Crisis

La Platte River Marsh, The Nature Conservancy

In 1864, George Perkins Marsh wrote *Man and Nature*, in which he discerned, "Man is everywhere a disturbing agent. Wherever he plants his foot, the harmonies of Nature are turned to discords." Youthful experiences in his native Vermont, followed by a lifetime of observation, led Marsh to express dismay at the human ignorance responsible for the abuse and deterioration of the land.

To sustain a healthy environment, Marsh believed we must become more knowledgeable about the natural world, realize the consequences of our actions, and exercise self-control. Today, more than ever, we need enlightened understanding of the interdependency of all living things. Even the preservation of a habitat where violets grow is related to our own survival.

Violets, Roaring Branch, Green Mountain National Forest

Hiking slowly through the crusted snow, we imagine Silas Lapham Griffith, Vermont's first millionaire, riding a horse-drawn carriage up this road to his summer home.

Eerie snaps and groans echo through the surrounding woods as we approach Griffith Lake. In the open expanse of solid blue sky and frozen lake, a thick cover of ice buckles from the sun's warmth, causing pressure cracks to shoot loudly from shore to shore.

Griffith Lake, White Rocks National Recreation Area

The falls are impressive from afar: an immense, dark cliff covered with moss and luxuriant growth, illuminated by the white froth of downpouring water. As if a tear in the sky had released its contents, the cascade splashes out of a tree-lined horizon, erupts over the first drop, then scatters down onto a succession of flat ledges. With atomized moisture swirling in the air, the shaded chasm is always a cool place.

Lye Brook Falls, Lye Brook Wilderness Area

A discreet path leads to a thirteen-acre stand of soaring white pines. Massive specimens like these were once marked by the British for their exclusive use as Royal Navy masts. The colonists rebelled against this foreign claim of ownership, believing the pines were theirs to cut. As a consequence of exploitation by many interests, the fabled forests were quickly logged. Groves of giant trees are gone, yet this hillside of tall, straight pines hints at the grandeur of the original virgin woods.

Canfield Fisher Memorial Pines, National Natural Landmark

Climbing Peru Peak in search of a view, we find instead a thickly forested summit, and a fascinating world at our feet.

The autumn carpet bursts nightly with colorful fungi, which decompose and recycle chemicals into the raw materials needed for next spring's leaves. Although it's dangerous to eat a wild mushroom without being absolutely certain of its identification, the cloverlike oxalis can be safely nibbled, added to salads, or steeped for a refreshing tea.

Forest Floor, Peru Peak Wilderness Area

"We should be impressed by the beauty and fragility of the dynamic balance that has been preserved for so many hundreds of millions of years during which life has *persisted* on earth. And we should especially appreciate the shortness of our tenure on earth and use the powers we have so recently assumed to perpetuate, not destroy, the balance."

ELIOT PORTER
Appalachian Wilderness: The Great Smoky Mountains

Beaver Channel at Dusk, George D. Aiken Wilderness Area

SPONSORS

The authors and the publisher gratefully acknowledge the following sponsors for their strong support and their financial assistance in helping to make the publication of this book possible:

The Vermont Natural Resources Council

Green Mountain Power Corporation

The authors and Storey Communications Inc. wish to thank several publishers for permission to quote from the following works:

Beston, Henry. *The Outermost House.* (New York: Rinehart, 1949). Courtesy Penguin USA.

Carson, Rachel. *The Sense of Wonder.* (New York: Harper & Row, 1965). Courtesy HarperCollins Publishers.

Douglas, William O. *This Is the American Earth.* (San Francisco: Sierra Club Books, 1960). Courtesy Sierra Club Books.

Eiseley, Loren. *The Firmament of Time.* (New York: Atheneum, 1960). Copyright © 1960 by Loren Eiseley; copyright © 1960 by the Trustees of the University of Pennsylvania. Courtesy Atheneum Publishers, an imprint of Macmillan Publishing Co.

Krutch, Joseph Wood. *Grand Canyon: Today and All Its Yesterdays.* (New York: William Sloane Associates, 1958). Courtesy William Morrow & Co., Inc.

Leopold, Aldo. *A Sand County Almanac.* (New York: Oxford University Press, 1949). Courtesy Oxford University Press.

Maxwell, Gavin. *Ring of Bright Water.* (New York: Dutton, 1960). Courtesy Penguin USA.

Platt, Rutherford. *The Great American Forest.* (Englewood Cliffs, New Jersey: Prentice Hall). Courtesy Prentice Hall Inc., a division of Simon and Schuster.

Porter, Eliot. *Appalachian Wilderness: The Great Smoky Mountains.* (New York: Dutton, 1970). Courtesy Penguin USA.

Teale, Edwin Way. *Dune Boy: The Early Years of a Naturalist.* (Bloomington, Indiana: Indiana University Press, 1986). Courtesy Indiana University Press.

Udall, Stuart. *The Quiet Crisis.* (New York: Holt, Rinehart and Winston, 1963). Courtesy Henry Holt & Co., Inc.

Wallace, David Rains. *Life in the Balance.* (Orlando, Florida: Harcourt Brace Jovanovich, 1987). Courtesy Harcourt Brace Jovanovich.